My Private Parts Belong to Me!

by Yael Feder

Illustrations: Lee Kurtzweil

From the Hebrew: Jessica Setbon

Schocken Children's Books

Hi! I'm Tammy and Guy's mother.

On Monday, Tammy and Guy came home from school and told me that the teacher had taught them about their bodies.
"Your bodies?" I asked.

"I'm a girl," said Tammy.
"And I'm a boy," said Guy. "There's a difference between boys and girls."
"I know that," I said. "Girls have long hair, and boys have short hair."

"No, Mom!" Tammy laughed. "Boys and girls have different private parts."

I didn't understand. "What are private parts?"
Tammy said that our body has some parts that are private and hidden. We keep these parts covered up, like with underwear or a bathing suit.
Tammy explained, "In front I have a private part that's called…"
"I know," I said. "Tootie!"
Tammy said, "The kids in class call it all kinds of nicknames, like 'front bottom' or 'hoo-hoo', but you can also say 'vagina'."

"Vagina?" I asked.
"Yes," Tammy said,
"and in back I have a…"
"I know - bottom!" I said enthusiastically.

"Right, bottom," Tammy replied. "But you can also call it 'buttocks'. That's the word the teacher taught us."
"That's right!" I smiled.
"I want to explain something else to you, Mom," said Tammy. "For girls, the chest is also a private part."

"So what does Guy have?" I asked.
"I have private parts, too," Guy said.

"In front I have a…"
"I know – weenie!" I said.
Guy laughed. "Mom, weenie sounds like a hot dog."
"So what's the right word for your private part?" I asked.
"You can call it 'penis'," Guy explained.
"I also have a private part in back that's called 'buttocks'."

But I didn't understand. "Why do they call those parts of your body 'private parts'?"

"They're called 'private parts' because they're private. They belong only to us, and no one else is allowed to touch them," Tammy and Guy continued.

But I didn't understand. "Nobody else is allowed to touch our private parts?"

Not Moms or Dads?
Not Grandmas or Grandpas?
Not brothers or sisters?
Or teachers?

Guy said that no one else is allowed to touch our private parts: not Mom or Dad, not Grandma or Grandpa. Not a brother or a sister, and not the teacher.

"Because my body belongs only to me," Tammy explained.

"So Daddy and I can't give you a bath?" I asked. Tammy laughed. "Of course you and Daddy can give us baths. You can also put on cream if my vagina itches, or wipe my bottom if I can't do it by myself.

Parents are allowed to help us do stuff so we'll stay clean and healthy."
"I get it," I said, relieved.

"Mom, do you know who else is not allowed to touch our private parts?" asked Guy.
"Who?" I said.
"Other kids," Guy explained. "Kids are not allowed to undress other kids or touch them on their private parts."

But I didn't understand. "So you can't play 'doctor' or 'house'?"

"Oh Mom, you're really mixed up! It's okay to play 'doctor' or to play 'house' – but without getting undressed and without touching the private parts: penis, vagina, breasts, and buttocks," said Guy.

"But what if you allow someone else to touch you?" I asked.

"Even if I allow it, it's not okay for someone else to touch my private parts," said Guy.
"Even if you're just playing a game?" I asked.
"Even if it's just a game, no one's allowed to touch my private parts and no one's allowed to undress," said Tammy.

But I didn't understand. "Even a real doctor is not allowed to touch our private parts?"

"When we don't feel well and we go to the doctor, the doctor needs to check us so he can help us and make us feel better," Tammy explained.

"Don't you remember, Mom? When my bottom hurt, you took me to the doctor, and the doctor checked my bottom and gave me a cream."

If I didn't let him check my private part, how could he help me?"
"Right," I said. "I didn't think of that…"

"The doctor's allowed to check us, but just to check and that's all – even if sometimes we feel uncomfortable," said Guy. "He has to find out what the problem is so he can help us. But we never go to the doctor by ourselves. We always go together with an adult – Mom or Dad, Grandma or Grandpa."

"But what if someone else does something else to my body that makes me uncomfortable?"

"If someone does something that makes us feel uncomfortable, like pinching us, or hitting us, then we have to say that we don't like it," Guy explained. "We have to say, 'No!' That's what the teacher said."

"And we run away as fast as a rabbit!" they both said, and raced around the table.

"Ah, now I get it. If someone does something bad to me, something that's not allowed, then I have to yell, 'No!' in a loud voice and run away."

"But do I need to tell someone about it?"

"Yes, Mommy. We have to tell an adult who can help," said Tammy. "Because if we don't tell, how can we get help?"

"But what if that person tells me that it's a secret? What if they tell me not to tell?"

"There are good secrets, and bad secrets," Guy explained. "A good secret is a secret about something good that happened. Remember when Daddy, Tammy and me made you a surprise party, Mom? We didn't tell you, so that we could surprise you. That's a good secret – something that makes you feel good. It's okay to keep that kind of a secret. If we had told you, you wouldn't have been surprised."

"That party was a wonderful surprise, and the mud pie you made for me was so delicious," I said. "Good thing you kept it a secret and didn't let it slip."

"But what's a bad secret?" I asked.

"A bad secret," said Guy, "is a secret about something bad that happened. It's a secret that makes us feel bad.

"If someone hits us,
or says something mean to us,
or scares us;
if someone wants to touch our private parts,
or wants us to touch their private parts – that's a bad secret.
When it's a bad secret, we have to tell. We have to! Even if someone tells us not to! Because if we tell someone, then they can help us."

"Right," Tammy added. "There's nothing to be afraid of. We have to tell. We have to be brave like lions!"

I still didn't understand. "But who do we tell a bad secret to?"

"To anyone who can help us," said Guy.

"Mommy

or Daddy,

Grandma

or Grandpa.

Your big brother

or an aunt,

a neighbor

or a teacher,

a police officer..."

"or even the President!"

Tammy said with a laugh.

"And then what happens?" I asked.

"After we tell the bad secret to a grownup, they believe us. They keep us safe and help us," Guy explained.
Now everything was clear. I wanted to hug Guy and Tammy really tight – my wonderful, smart kids.
But then I got confused again.

"I understand that my body belongs only to me, and your bodies belong only to you. So from now on, Daddy and I can't hug and kiss you?"

"Of course you're allowed to hug us! Of course you're allowed to kiss us, if you want! 'Cause it's good and fun to snuggle up close with someone you love," said Tammy and Guy, and they laughed.

Dear parents,

This book teaches children how to protect their bodies and their privacy. In a friendly and direct style that is age appropriate, it explains to the young readers how to avoid abuse, and what to do in case there is an attempt for abuse.

Despite our efforts as parents to protect our children from any harm, every child is exposed to the danger of sexual abuse. Most cases of abuse are carried out by a person that the child knows: a family member, a friend, neighbor, or babysitter. Most children don't talk about it. Therefore often adults who care for the child are responsible to discover signs of abuse.

If you suspect that abuse has taken place, you should speak with the child using terms from his or her daily life. Let the child tell what happened at his or her own pace. Avoid closed questions (with "yes" or "no" answers). Instead, allow the child to express his or her story freely. Stay calm, since an emotional reaction on your part is likely to scare the child, intensify any feelings of guilt, and shut down communication. Show the child that you trust what he or she is telling and that you are listening carefully. Reassure the child that he or she is brave for telling what happened and that he or she should not take the burden of the secret alone any more.

The child is always the victim of the abuse – never the cause. In most cases, children experience strong feelings of guilt, so tell the child directly that what happened was not his or her fault. Verify that you have understood all the details in the child's story correctly, but try to minimize the number of times the story is repeated. To help the child regain sense of control, explain to the child the next steps in the process such as getting physical and emotional help, contacting the authorities etc.

If you think the child was abused, it's important to contact professionals to get advice and treatment, and to report to the relevant authorities.

Sharona Ariel, social worker, Yael's Friends Theater Company

Yael Feder
My Private Parts Belong to Me!

1 2 3 4 5 6 7 8 9 1 0

This publication or any part thereof may not be reproduced, photographed, recorded, broadcasted, translated, scanned, stored in a database, or distributed in any form or by any electronic or mechanical means, including the internet, electronic book, computer, tablet, cellphone or other media format, without the written permission of the publisher.

Copyright by Schocken Publishing House Ltd., Tel Aviv
Design: Avigayil Sagi
www.schocken.co.il
Arranged by Schocken Publishing House, 2019
ISBN 978-965-19-1071-5

To my beloved family:
Yuval, Amit, Tamar, Michal and Dani